Commuting a Life Sentence to Time Served

Finding Hope and Healing Through Divorce

Holly S. Ross

Commuting a Life Sentence to Time Served:
Finding Hope and Healing Through Divorce
Copyright © 2024 Holly S. Ross

Produced and printed by Stillwater River Publications. All rights reserved. Written and produced in the United States of America. This book may not be reproduced or sold in any form without the expressed, written permission of the author(s) and publisher.

Visit our website at **www.StillwaterPress.com** for more information.

First Stillwater River Publications Edition

ISBN: 978-1-965733-03-5

1 2 3 4 5 6 7 8 9 10

Publisher's Cataloging-in-Publication
Provided by Cassidy Cataloguing Services, Inc.

Names: Ross, Holly S., author.
Title: Commuting a life sentence to time served : finding hope and healing through divorce / Holly S. Ross.
Description: First Stillwater River Publications edition. | West Warwick, RI, USA : Stillwater River Publications, [2025]
Identifiers: ISBN: 978-1-965733-03-5
Subjects: LCSH: Divorce—Psychological aspects. | Marriage—Psychological aspects. | Divorce—Humor. | Marriage—Humor. | LCGFT: Self-help publications. | Essays.
Classification: LCC: HQ814 .R67 2025 | DDC: 306.89—dc23

Written by Holly S. Ross.
Cover and interior design by Elisha Gillette.
Published by Stillwater River Publications, West Warwick, RI, USA.

The views and opinions expressed in this book are solely those of the author(s) and do not necessarily reflect the views and opinions of the publisher.

I dedicate this book of essays to my family and friends who were there when I needed them the most; you know who you are.

Table of Contents

Introduction	1	Walking Away a Winner		
Embrace Inspiration	3	(Find Your Theme Song)	35	
One Size Doesn't Fit Everyone	4	On the Flip Side	36	
Accepting Grace	5	Just Skip It	38	
Making It Real	6	Milestones and Millstones	39	
I Wouldn't… But I Guess I Did	7	Four-Fifths of the Way There	40	
The Other Horton Story	9	Never Forget	41	
South Pacific	10	Unraveling the Past	43	
You Are Worthy	11	A New Superpower!	44	
Pick a Word, Any Word	12	Exchanging Piece of Mind		
Wishing You Dog Days	14	for Peace of Mind	45	
Forgive? Are You Crazy?	16	Don't Fence Me In!	47	
Reclaiming Your Identity	18	Mandated Etiquette	49	
Pronouns	20	Mountains…….	50	
Simple Joys	21	And Molehills….	51	
Arithmetic	22	Getting to the Root of Things	52	
No More Excuses	24	Old Book Sale	54	
Life Is Not a Hallmark Movie	25	Gold Stars	55	
Airing Things Out	27	A Cup of Love	57	
If Not in This Life….	28	And Hugs….	58	
Losing Those Extra Pounds	29	Ink Spots	59	
Silence Is Golden	30	Trying to Remember	61	
Going Out on a Limb	31	Yet…	62	
Recipe for Lemonade	32	"What's Stopping You?"	64	
Contrary to Popular Advice…		Out of Our Control	66	
Don't Look Up!	33	But Not Out of Control…	68	
		A Cracked Pot	70	

Sage Advice	71	The Key	100
Pruning for New Growth	72	Alone Does Not Have to Mean Lonely	102
Waves	74		
Card-Carrying?	76	Labels	104
Calculus—and More!	77	Laughter Crowds out Pain and Anger	105
Dreaded Day?	79		
Stick a Pin in It!	80	Celebration!	107
I Am Enough…Not!	81	Braking for the Future	108
Symbols	83	Ready…? Or Not…?	109
A Little Nutty	85	Stage Production	110
Lists	87	Seeking...	111
Yes, You Can	89	And Persuing...	112
A New Coat	91	On and On and On and On….	113
Don't Go There	93	My Benediction (= Good Words) to You	115
OCD…. or CDO….or COD	94		
Personal Growth	96		
Food for Thought	98	*About the Author*	*116*

Introduction

WHO WOULD HAVE THOUGHT THAT AFTER FORTY years of marriage I would be in the throes of a divorce? Not I. I had made a lifetime commitment and although it wasn't the marriage I had hoped and planned, I had carved out a life where I could find some joy and a sense of fulfillment.

Then one day in December my husband told me that he was going to seek out a counselor. For the first time in years, I felt a sense of hope. Twenty-four hours later, that hope was dashed when he told me he had spent two and a half hours with his lawyers that day…and he wanted "an amicable separation and divorce." I asked him the one (rhetorical) question I knew in my heart I had to ask: "You don't want to work on the marriage?" With a look in his eyes I'll never forget, he said emphatically, "NO!" And that was that. There were no tears—that would come later—in regard to how it affected others in the family.

Looking back, I should have seen the signs…all along the way, but I wanted and expected things to work out. God knows I tried.

Now what was I supposed to do? This devotional book arose out of that questioning time and the "thought of the day" which was brought to me each morning by way of God's angels. If you, too, find yourself in this club that you never thought you would "join," I pray that my experience and insights may help bring light and healing to you.

"One day you will tell your story of how you overcame what you went through and it will be someone else's survival guide."

—Brene Brown

May this be your survival guide.

—HSR

Embrace Inspiration

A WORD. A SONG. A PAINTING. A PHRASE. A COOKIE (Yes, even a cookie!) A photo. An aroma. A texture. A movie. A post on Facebook.

The list could go on for a long time. What do they have in common? They all can be sources of inspiration for you on your new journey.

The title of this collection of essays came to me one morning before my feet even landed on the floor. "Commuting a life sentence to time served." Now where did that come from? I wrote it down on one of the index cards that I had placed on my night table for just such a purpose. The rest of the day that phrase kept coming to the forefront of my mind—and it made me smile. It was time to move ahead with the rest of my life. As I looked out on the vast expanse of my life which lay before me, I knew in the depths of my soul not only that I could move on, I would move on.

I embraced that saying with my whole being. Later, when I met with my attorney, I shared that phrase with her and told her I didn't have a copyright on it; to go ahead and share with any of her clients who might need a word or two of encouragement!

And so began these daily bits of inspiration. Where did they come from? God? Spirit? Angels? Subconscious? You can decide that for yourself. For me, it was a lifeline thrown to me from the Source of All Love. And once I had these thoughts, I knew they were meant not only for me, but for all who are in search of healing and hope as they navigate these new waters of divorce and what's next. Embrace inspiration for what it is—a gift of love and support.

One Size Doesn't Fit Everyone

THIS COLLECTION OF ESSAYS IS JUST THAT—thoughts that helped me along the way from that shocking first declaration that he wanted a divorce to finding a place of hope and healing. It is a collection. It is in no particular order. If the particular "thought of the day" doesn't resonate with you, skip to the next day or randomly open this book and read whatever your finger falls on. These are essays. The word comes from the French, meaning "attempt" or "try." As I was attempting to see myself through the myriad thoughts and fears and dreams and disappointments, anger and resignation, I realized that others were in similar places. But my story is not your story.

When an article of clothing would say, "one size fits all," my mother used to comment, "It fits where it touches." Not everything I will share will fit you and your situation. How could it? But my prayer is that some of these will touch your heart when and how you need it.

So my thought for the day today is:

"What lies behind you
And what lies ahead of you
Pales in comparison to
What lies inside you."

—Ralph Waldo Emerson

Accepting Grace

WHEN I TRY TO RECONSTRUCT THOSE FIRST FEW days after he told me he wanted a divorce, I am at a loss. All the days and times blur together. Looking back, I would say I was in shock. I don't recall the conversations I had with my sons, but I do remember them showing up—with boxes (to pack up his stuff and to rid my house of his presence) and food (who wanted to eat?) and kids (to help me immerse myself in their love and joy) and energy. None of which I seemed to have or was able to summon out of the depths of my being.

They took down pictures and plaques and old gutters.

They prepared food and "encouraged" (read "made") me eat something.

They told me to take care of myself.

They gave me practical advice, like start exercising every day, and make a cup of tea each day and sit down with it and put up my feet.

They made all the arrangements for me to spend a week in Florida with them and took care of all the expenses and travel.

They made sure I wasn't alone on the holidays.

My sisters and aunt checked in on me often and visited in person and/or by phone. Friends I had made through the years texted me and listened.

How can I possibly pay them back for throwing me a lifeline when I felt like I was sinking into an abyss? I can't. I had to learn to accept this grace in my life and thank God for sending these angels, these messengers, of love and hope. I wish you angels in your life.

Making It Real

IN THE BEGINNING, IT JUST DIDN'T SEEM REAL. Was I really going to be divorced?

The first person I told in person that my husband had asked me for a divorce responded by laughing in my face. Needless to say, I was taken aback. Eventually I responded, "Well, that's an odd reaction." She stopped laughing.

I shouldn't be so hard on her, I suppose. She was laughing in disbelief, probably. I don't know. I didn't ask her. But part of me could definitely relate. It didn't seem real, even (or especially) to me.

Approximately twenty-seven years earlier he had mentioned getting a divorce. I remember the shock then, too. That time, however, I cried and begged him to reconsider. My sons were in elementary school. My employment was tied to his. I had no place to go. I was afraid.

He didn't mention it again, as I said, for twenty-seven years. I didn't have the courage then to ask what—or who—he wanted instead. This time I realized I didn't care.

But it still seemed surreal.

So, despite the laughing reaction I received from that first person, I went on to tell more and more people. Surprisingly, it helped me to grasp the reality of it all. I needed to acknowledge what was really happening this time. I needed to "own" this new fact of life so I could deal with all the details to come—and move ahead.

There would be no going back.

I Wouldn't...
But I Guess I Did

SHOPPING IN THE STORE I USED TO WORK IN, I RAN into a man who is a frequent shopper there. "You're back!" he said, smiling. "No," I replied, shaking my head, "I'm not back…the divorce is final." A married man for perhaps as long—or longer—than I had been, he uttered those words I am still trying to figure out how best to respond to: "I'm sorry." My filter down, I quipped, "I won't stay with someone who doesn't want me!"

I was quite satisfied with my answer…until I was driving home. It hit me that for those twenty-seven intervening years between his first declaration of wanting a divorce and his second, I just might have been living with a man who didn't want me.

I was still conducting a postmortem on my marriage. I think I still am.

A friend asked me how I could stay in the marriage after the first declaration. There is no easy answer to that. I don't remember exactly what triggered his desire for a divorce; the best I can do is recall that I had said something about his mother's poor choices, yet she was still alive, and my mom, who had none of his mother's bad habits, had died.

You don't say anything negative about his mother. So, I never did again. I put my head down and forged ahead, trying my best to make a warm and loving home for my sons. I carved out my own niche and lived in it. I threw myself into my boys' activities, my career, and my hobbies. I refused to think about the status of my marriage.

That is hardly the advice I would give to anyone, but to be honest, that's what I did. If I had to do it over again, I'm not sure what I would do.

The Other Horton Story

DR. SEUSS. PEOPLE SEEM TO EITHER LOVE HIS STORIES or hate them. I fall into the first category. Over the decades his rhyming books have taught countless kids how to read. But the stories I love best teach us about our world and how to live in it. *The Lorax* is on my short list of favorite stories of all times, teaching environmentalism in a way everyone can understand. And *Horton Hears a Who* tells us that "a person's a person, no matter how small."

But what about the other Horton story? It really resonates with me.

Have you read *Horton Hatches the Egg*? The theme: "An elephant's faithful 100 percent." The premise is that the mother bird wants a break from sitting on her egg, so she asks Horton the elephant to keep the egg warm—just a short break, she says. Well, she doesn't come back and she doesn't come back and Horton is left sitting on the egg through storms and cold and heat....

As with most "children's" stories, we don't question the plausibility of an elephant sitting on a bird's egg in a tree for a year, and I don't want to ruin the end of the story for those who haven't read it yet, but genetics is thrown to the wind, too. However, the faithfulness and commitment of Horton the elephant is never in question. And, (spoiler alert) his faithfulness is rewarded in the end.

In my own way, I tried for years to weather the storms and be the anchor of our home. I don't have to look far to see that my faithfulness paid off in the end. Mind you, my marriage had a surprise ending, but to see my sons, I know my faithfulness has paid off, 100 percent.

South Pacific

WAKING ONE MORNING, I HAD A SONG FROM *South Pacific* looping in my brain. To be honest, I don't remember ever seeing this musical, but somehow I "heard" "Gonna Wash That Man Right out of My Hair" over and over and over, like an earworm.

Was there a message there?

I started formulating a plan….

The figurative expression was to become a literal experience! With my life turned upside down, I needed to turn other aspects of my life on their "heads." Why not start at the top! I wanted a new look. I wanted something dramatic, but not permanent. Nothing like a tattoo or piercing. "Act in haste, repent in leisure" was an expression I had already experienced in my life.

So I made an appointment at my hairdresser's and told her I wanted a CHANGE! So a few days later I came out of the salon with a very curly permanent (which of course it isn't!) and some highlights!

Change CAN be good…but often in order to feel good, we have to feel like we are the ones controlling our future.

Take baby steps.

Speaking from my experience, my new "look" gave me a new outlook and a feeling I had a grasp on the next chapter of my life.

You Are Worthy

A FRIEND OF MINE ONCE DESCRIBED DATING AS A series of rejecting and being rejected. With twenty-twenty hindsight the red flags are frantically waving at us in semaphore that the one who just rejected us is one we should have rejected!

But rejection is hard, whether we are on the giving or receiving end. None of us is perfect and if love isn't blind, it at least needs glasses. "Why didn't you warn me?" someone asked me. I took it as a rhetorical question. We make our own choices and at certain points in our relationships we don't want to have the negative pointed out to us, now do we? Stumbling blocks look like mere imperfections. This person has CHOSEN me. What greater compliment is given than for someone to say they want to spend the rest of their lives with you? It gives you a great sense of worth. "I am worthy! Worthy of love and acceptance and a happily ever after."

Now we have to deal with rejection. Whether it is after four months, four years or forty years…it hurts. Even when you arrive where everyone else is—that you should have rejected that person from the very beginning—it still hurts. No one likes rejection.

But you are worthy. You always have been and always will be worthy.

I am a child of God.
I am made in God's image.
I have the spark of God's light within me and God wants me to let it shine.
I am worthy.
(Repeat.)

Pick a Word, Any Word

WHEN YOUR WORLD HAS JUST BEEN TURNED ON its side, just getting through each day can be a daunting task.

For me, I turned to some pewter inspirational shapes I had collected over the years and put them in a very small basket within reach of my bed. I could just reach out and pick one piece and declare that was the "word of the day"; that which would inspire me or encourage me or just get me through my next waking moments.

Imagine…believe…breathe…happiness….faith…joy…sparkle…courage…hope…giggle…love…dream…peace…play…. Lastly, a picture of an angel.

Whichever word I pulled, I would hold it and think on it for a few moments. The last thing I would do after I got dressed was to slip that little bit of metal in my pocket. Sometimes I would pull it out during the day; other times I would just run my fingers over it. On good days, I forgot about it altogether because it had already seeped into my soul for the day. On more than one occasion I found one in the bottom of my washing machine; those times would make me smile as I retrieved the errant token and lovingly placed it back in the basket.

Of course, the same can be done with slips of paper placed in a jar. I liked the pewter because it symbolized permanence to me, that good things were in my life or soon would be or I should strive to make them be. And even a good spin through the washer couldn't take away those positive messages!

And now, dear brothers and sisters, one final thing. Fix your thoughts on what is true, and honorable, and right, and pure, and lovely, and admirable. Think about things that are excellent and worthy of praise.

—Philippians 4:8

Wishing You Dog Days

WE ALL NEED A REASON TO GET OUT OF BED IN the morning—more than just getting up to use the facilities. We all know that after that you can easily just crawl back into bed and pull the blankets over your head. I wish for you to have dog days.

Fortunately, I have a dog, a greyhound to be more specific. My dog doesn't ask much from me, but he creates a reason to get up—and dressed—in the morning: he must be fed and walked. And then once I am up, I start my day with a cup of coffee.

Perhaps you have a job. Good. That gives you a reason to rouse yourself and present yourself to the world, even if it is remotely via Zoom. When my ex decided he wanted a divorce he also took away my job (in the family business) and my work and worship at my church (where he also worked and worshipped). He tried to claim dual custody of the dog. That's the line I wasn't going to cross. No surprise to those who know me and how loving animals is at the core of my being. Dogs get you up in the morning and keep you going through the rough days.

The dog days of summer are the hottest days of the year. No matter what the season, you are in some of the hottest, most turbulent days of your life. Don't despair. Find what brings you joy, like the warmth of a cuddling dog who senses your distress, and lean into it. Dog days aren't bad; they are different. Celebrate what you can, when you can!

(Note: If you don't have a dog, now is probably not the best time to acquire one. You have to take care of yourself and that's hard enough when you're hurting without taking on more responsibility. But perhaps you have children! My sons are grown, but if you have kids in the house, they certainly will give you a reason to get up and going! But the flip side is just as important: you need not only to be strong for them, but you need to carve out time for self-care.)

Forgive? Are You Crazy?

IT HADN'T EVEN BEEN A MONTH SINCE THE "DEClaration" and subsequent move out of the house, when I was on a much-needed vacation with my younger son and his girlfriend and her kids. A change of scenery and warm weather and great company was helping start the process of examining life in general and my new role in it in particular.

It was then that a very well-meaning, new person in my life gave me a gift—a book she had picked up in a thrift store. Being twice divorced herself, she thought this would be a good book for me. As graciously as I could, I thanked her for it and put it in my suitcase to take home. Once I was home, I unpacked the book and placed it on my bookshelf. Where it still sits today…unread. I still might open the cover one day, but that day is not yet.

The title of the book? It is one of the Chicken Soup for the Soul books—*The Power of Forgiveness: 101 Stories about How to Let Go & Change Your Life*.

Forgiveness is so often misunderstood. I had the academic knowledge that forgiveness isn't so much about the person who has betrayed you, as it is about releasing you from the negative energy that surrounds you.

Well, that sounds all well and good, but when it comes down to it, it is very difficult to really do. What can make it even harder to do is when the offender doesn't ask for forgiveness, nor even acknowledge their behavior in the first place! They don't even know that you are grappling with embracing forgiveness; in their mind, they have done nothing wrong, so forgiveness doesn't need to be sought!

I have been able to get to the point where if he reaches the point of trying to make amends, I will listen. But to promise forgiveness is a stretch at this point.

As an ordained minister, some would say that I am in the forgiveness "business." How can I urge others to forgive, when I haven't "gotten there" myself? Well, mea culpa. I'm working on it. But I can tell you that there is no hate in my heart….and right now that is the best I can do.

Reclaiming Your Identity

FROM THE TIME I CAN REMEMBER, WRITING thank you notes was ingrained in me every time I received a gift. My mother taught me the basics: heading, salutation, three paragraphs (three sentences in each paragraph), closing, and signature. In some cases (where I really didn't like the gift or it didn't fit me) my creative writing skills were honed. Then there was the envelope. Mr. and Mrs., or Mr. or Miss or Mrs. (This was the age before Ms.)

When my great uncle died, I was about to address the envelope to my great aunt as Mrs. Jean. I was quickly informed that that was a great faux pas! She was still Mrs. John. Mrs. Jean would imply that she was divorced, not widowed…

When I was no longer under the watchful eye of my mother, I dropped all titles and prefixes. Envelopes were addressed to First name Last name. Even in the beginning of my marriage when I was still starry-eyed, I cringed when letters came addressed to me as Mrs. His first name His last name. Where had my identity gone?!!! And when I earned my master of divinity degree, and letters came addressed to The Rev. Mrs. His first name His last name, I felt like even my accomplishment lay hidden behind his name.

So when he asked for a divorce one of the positive aspects that came to light was that I could once again claim my identity! Now, my mother had instilled in me that "one doesn't change their name, they merely add to it," and I had used my maiden name as my middle name and always signed documents with it, but to most people, it was lost. Now divorced, I can honestly say that I can take or leave my title—as the Rev. or as Ms.—but reverting to my maiden name gives me a sense of who I authentically am.

Reclaim who you really are—proclaim it to all who will listen!

Pronouns

IT WAS AN INNOCENT ENOUGH QUESTION. WE were just making small talk. "When did such and such happen?" she asked. "We…." And I could go no further—it were as if time stopped and all the "we" moments came flooding to my mind. I tried to shake it off and return to the conversation. Opening my mouth, I heard myself say, "I…." Then continued my thought…filling in the silence.

But the "we/I, us/me, our/my" quandary persisted. The past was "we" and "us" and "our." There was no denying that. But to voice those pronouns gave me a twinge in my heart. The dreams I had always held of a marriage of mutual love and respect and support had been dashed on the rocks of divorce and there was no turning back the clock. With that twinge came a smidge of the old sense of failure.

There. I said it. Looking into the future there might never be a "we" or "us" or "our" moment again in my life. Divorced and alone. I'm not much into wallowing in self-pity. Oh, a moment or two, sure. But once I indulged in those moments, I started looking for my bootstraps by which to pull myself out of the mire.

Pronouns…they had put my life into perspective. But what are pronouns except words that take the place of nouns—of people. The "we," "us," or "our" moments of the future might not be with a sweetheart, but rather with close family and friends…perhaps even new friends with shared interests. I do believe that we are not meant to be alone, but that doesn't mean we have to be in a "relationship" as defined by Facebook! Let's embrace life with the people around us, sharing life's great adventure! We can do it!

Simple Joys

SO...WHAT IS ON YOUR BUCKET LIST?

I have some complex and costly things on my list, but just the other day I achieved one goal. And it only cost me some birdseed.

That's right—actual birdseed. I saw that a friend of mine had posted a video of her feeding chickadees right out of her hand. Now that is one thing I always wanted to do. Several years ago I put a red glove on the deck railing with birdseed in the palm of the glove. I figured the birds needed to get used to the idea of eating off a glove. However, I never followed up on that project. I thought it would take hours of sitting in the cold—frozen stiff.

Encouraged by my friend's success, I sat out on my folding chair for twenty minutes...without success. I checked in with her and she told me to sit right next to the feeder (the first time I had been sitting about twenty feet away from it). I sat still with sunflower seeds in my outstretched glove and lo and behold, it wasn't even five minutes before a chickadee ate out of my hand. And again...and again...and again....

Now I had no one there to take a picture, never mind a video, but I knew what had just happened and the smile on my face didn't fade for about an hour. What a simple, yet profound joy.

So what does this have to do with finding hope and healing through divorce? Just a reminder—for everyone—to find those simple joys in life and revel in the rapture that comes with them. For that is what life is really all about.

Arithmetic

WHAT IS THE FIRST MATH PROBLEM YOU EVER solved? One plus one equals two, right?

So why do people often refer to their "life partner" as their better half? Doesn't that seem to imply that the equation has shifted from "one plus one equals two" to "one half plus one half equals one"?

Where does that idea come from? Perhaps it is from the New Testament of the Bible: Mark 10:7-8 (and Ephesians 5:31.) "For this reason a man shall leave his father and mother and be joined to his wife, and the two shall become one flesh. So they are no longer two, but one flesh." (NRSV) Now when I first read that as a young teen, I thought it was pretty racy; that they were referring to copulation. But the point Jesus was making is really found in the next verse: "Therefore what God has joined together, let no one separate." Jesus was elevating a woman's role in a marriage to that of an equal partner.

But that is lost on most people, and so, the arithmetic changes and people are thought of as "halves" in a marriage. And comments like "He completes me" arise.

I'm sure the comments are well intentioned, but still, they are misguided.

To enter any healthy relationship, each person must come as a whole human being—warts and all, yes, but not leaning on the other to find fulfillment. Otherwise, disappointment and heartache are sure to follow…eventually.

And if the relationship dissolves, the arithmetic goes from addition to subtraction.

Will it be "two minus one equals one" or "one minus one half equals one half"?

May we all realize our worth as whole human beings, worthy of love and respect.

No More Excuses

I FIND THAT WE FIND TIME TO DO THOSE THINGS that we really want to do.

Early in my ministry, I recall trying to schedule a meeting. I asked one of the farmers in the congregation when the best time would be to have it and he shared, "You know, if there is a farm auction, farmers schedule their chores so they can get there. You choose the time that works for you, and if they want to come, they will be there."

We all have the same twenty-four hours in each day. How we spend it is up to us.

Something I have always wanted to do was to take bagpipe lessons. I started when my firstborn was about a year old…then the teacher got sick and I moved. Decades passed and a chance encounter led me to a piper who taught in the next town. And I was taking lessons again!

However, I wasn't as dedicated as I should have been to practicing. In my mind I found many excuses, including not bothering the other person in the house with my amateurish squeaks and squawks. I told myself that he didn't support my efforts. Truth be told, I don't think he cared one way or another.

So, now there are no more excuses. My success—or failure—in this venture (and others!) lies with me.

Watch out world, the piping is about to begin!

Life Is Not a Hallmark Movie

MUCH LIKE BAGPIPE MUSIC, PEOPLE FALL INTO two camps in regard to Hallmark movies: those who love them and those who can't stand them.

I had always been in the former group. There was always something very reassuring about watching one of these signature movies. The plot was always the same. Boy meets girl. They hit it off. Then there is some kind of misunderstanding. Then they patch it up and they live happily ever after. Wrapped up in a nice little package, it was a predictable gift of two hours of escapism and it left you feeling all warm and fuzzy.

When the reality of my impending divorce hit me, I found myself suddenly in the latter group. There are no "happily ever afters" in life. We have been deluded by the movie industry. Life is not that predictable. These were the thoughts that whirled in my head.

Then I remembered my parents. They were each other's best friend. They supported each other's dreams and goals and ambitions. Maybe life isn't all sweetness and light all the time, but for some, there can be mutual love and respect and joy.

And so I started watching Hallmark movies again. They do provide escapism and something to keep me company while I am knitting up my latest project. They do not reflect life as I know it, but that's okay—I also like to watch shows about UFOs and ghosts. They aren't everyone's reality, but they give me something else to think about!

May you find something to captivate your thoughts—if even for only an hour or two! Life might not be a Hallmark movie, but you can dream!

Airing Things Out

ONE OF MY FAVORITE AROMAS IS THE FLEETING smell of spring. If you have ever smelled it, you know what I mean. If you have never experienced it, I cannot explain it to you.

I was changing the sheets on my bed the other day and the linens that I pulled from my cabinet smelled like what they were: sheets that had sat too long without having seen the light of day. I hung them outside on the railing of my deck for only an hour or two. And voila! They smelled like the outdoors!

And that brought back wonderful memories of my childhood. We never had a dryer growing up, so Saturday morning was the day we washed our laundry and hung it on the lines to dry. Then that night I would snuggle down in bed and deeply breathe in the fresh aroma.

So my mind wandered to the saying about "airing one's dirty laundry." Yuck. But what about airing one's laundry in whatever condition it is in?

I hope you find a friend (or friends) like I did, to whom you can pour out your heart, share stories—good and bad, even those memories you forced into the recesses of your mind. Shaking them out and letting fresh air blow through them will help you heal and find light and laughter again.

I promise.

There is immeasurable goodness and joy out there. Don't let the past define your future. Fresh winds are blowing!

If Not in This Life….

THIS WEEK I RECEIVED MY MEDICARE CARD. I AM now officially "old." I can no longer honestly say that I am middle-aged. (I clung to that terminology for longer than I should have, I know.)

Over the hill…coasting downhill…best years behind me….

Now isn't that all depressing? Not necessarily.

I was talking with a dear friend not long ago, bemoaning the poor choices I had made that landed me where I was today relationship-wise. In other words, nowhere. It was at that point in time that I began hoping for reincarnation. Maybe I had learned enough lessons in this life that, if given another chance, I could find true love and maybe even passion.

Now stop laughing.

"It's not the number of breaths we take;

it is the number of moments that take our breath away."

This phrase found popularity many years ago, but its truth is timeless. No matter how young or old you are, there is still time in this lifetime, to find moments that take away our breath.

We just have to be open to it!

Now *go*!!! Find those moments!!!

Losing Those Extra Pounds

MANY PEOPLE ARE STRESS EATERS. WHEN THINGS are in turmoil, often we eat—or try to eat our way through those times. What often results is weight gain.

I was talking with a friend I had known for only a year who had been divorced several years ago. She is about my height and maybe a few pounds heavier than I, but when she mentioned losing 170 pounds after her divorce, I had trouble imagining her at more than double her current weight! One hundred seventy pounds is like another human being!!!!

Oh…right….

She "lost" another person….

Decades ago, another friend of mine actually DID lose a lot of weight over the summer on a diet plan and exercise. I ran into him in the grocery store after not seeing him all summer. When I remarked that he was looking great and that he must have lost a lot of weight, he commented that it shouldn't be called "losing" weight. "It isn't easy to do, like losing your car keys; it's hard work!"

Divorcing someone isn't easy. It's not like misplacing your car keys. In many ways it is hard work. However, if you are struggling to make things work with the person you are with, and counseling is no longer an option, it's time to lose the weight. It's hard work sometimes, but the end result is worth it—people will notice and comment on your beaming smile at what you have accomplished.

Silence Is Golden

SO WHEN HE MOVED OUT HE TOOK THE BRAND new HUGE television set with him. It had been the focal point of the living room. Now there was an empty space that seemed to loom over me. The TV, which had been on almost 24/7 when he was living in this house, had filled the silence that had come between us. Now there was nothing but the ticking of the clock.

I started sitting on the sectional in the place that looked out the window at the view of the lake and the mountains, rather than face the void. So, the optical problem was "fixed," but the silence ….

My thoughts seemed to be going 24/7 in much the way the TV had. Monologue that was filled with doubts and questions and what-ifs—until I could drift off into the same question-filled sleep and dreams that made no sense.

And then it happened.

I welcomed the silence as a respite from my chaotic life. It was soothing and appealing. It reached out to me, offering solace for my soul.

"Silence is golden," my mom would say as we were growing up. I didn't understand it at the time. When the TV would be turned off or the radio would go silent or my sisters and I would stop arguing, my mother would heave a great sigh of relief and declare, "Silence is golden!"

Finally I understood. Silence is not the enemy. Silence can soothe jangled nerves. Silence can help us take a break and relax. Silence can bring us that inner peace we cannot find in the noise that surrounds much of our lives. It is a gift that no money can buy. Silence is golden.

Going Out on a Limb

WHEN I RECEIVED MY FIRST CAMERA AS A CHILD, I took a myriad of pictures of our cats, the neighbor's dogs, trees, and places of historic interest. Rarely did I take pictures of family, and even more infrequently did I take pictures of friends! Subconsciously I think I rationalized that they would always be there, but the colors of the leaves on the trees were always changing, so I had to capture that on film. Pets had relatively short lifespans, so I needed to document their lives. And when would I be back at Lincoln's birthplace? But family and friends? I could always take their picture another day.

Growing up, I didn't have a large family. I had parents and two sisters. My father was an only child and my mother only had one sister. I have two first cousins. Four grandparents and a smattering of great aunts and great uncles and a few more distant cousins we saw on occasion. Some of those still alive, I am in contact with, thanks mostly to social media.

However, going through this divorce, I am appreciating my extended family more than ever. Thanks to 23andMe, I have discovered and rediscovered cousins far and wide! My family tree has sprouted new branches and I am enjoying going out on these new limbs. Of course, with some, I am not able to make connections, but I am thankful for every connection I do make.

This summer, I will be meeting some of my relatives for the first time. I have talked on the phone with some. I just might have to make plans for road trips to meet others. It will all be worth it because "blessed be the tie that binds our hearts" through bloodlines!

Recipe for Lemonade

WE HAVE ALL SEEN THE SLOGAN, "WHEN LIFE GIVES you lemons, make lemonade!" However, I have yet to see the corollary that gives you a recipe for the lemonade!

So, here is a recipe I found: "Boil for five minutes: two cups of sugar and one cup of water with the rinds of three lemons cut into thin strips. Let the syrup cool and add the juice of eight lemons. Strain and store in a covered container in the refrigerator. Use two tablespoons of the syrup for every glass of ice water to make lemonade."

What can we extrapolate from this recipe for real life?

When life gets tough, we often have to be in hot water for a while until things get better.

We need to add more than twice the sweetness to counteract the bitterness of life.

We need to cut up our lives into manageable pieces.

We need to squeeze the negative things to the last drop…and figure out where to go from there.

Let things cool down before acting on anything, or we might be sorry later.

Things will keep; we don't need to do everything right now.

Dish things out as needed. It's okay to wait for the right time.

Life is made for sharing with family and friends. Sitting on a porch, just enjoying each other's company, slowly sipping both the sweetness and acridness of life.

With time, we see that the lemons have given our lives sharper focus and the impetus to move ahead, growing into our full potential.

Contrary to Popular Advice... Don't Look Up!

HOW OFTEN HAVE YOU HEARD THESE WORDS OF encouragement: "Look up! Better days are coming!"?

Well, I'm telling you this: "When life is looking bleak and you wonder how you can possibly put one foot in front of the other, don't look up; look down!"

I am the youngest of three girls, and growing up, I often looked to my sisters for advice and encouragement. We traveled quite a bit as a family and we had to do quite a bit of walking to see the sights of wherever we might be on any given day. My sisters are three and six years older than I and it was often difficult for my little legs to keep up with the strides not only of my parents, but of my older siblings as well. This was especially true when climbing sets of stairs or hills. That is when the older of my older sisters offered these words which have served me well through the years: "Don't look up; look down at your feet and just keep going!"

Yes, by looking down, you only see a little piece of ground to cover at any one particular time. You don't get overwhelmed! And yes, you get where you are going.

Perhaps you are feeling overwhelmed at the moment by all the decisions you need to make, or the lack of control you have over what is happening in your life. "Look up!" some may tell you. "It will get better!" Well, life will get better…but if you look up, you may not find anything on which to rest your eyes. Nothing to give you direction… nothing to help you put one foot in front of the other.

So, look down. What is one small thing you can accomplish today? And then build on that one step tomorrow. It will get better…one small step at a time.

Walking Away a Winner (Find Your Theme Song)

TALKING WITH SEVERAL PEOPLE WHO HAVE BEEN through divorce themselves, I find that many of us found a theme song to carry us through the difficult times. For one it was "I Will Survive." For another, it was "I Am Woman." For me, it was—and is—Kathy Mattea's "Walking Away a Winner." As I play the CD cranked up to full volume, I am momentarily transported to another time and place—a place of power and control over an otherwise chaotic and turbulent time. I have even "perfected" hand motions to it as I belt it out at the top of my lungs!

Music has a way of empowering us. We realize that others have been in the same place that we are—people who came out okay (often better!) on the other side. Don't know a song to fit your situation? As cliché as it might seem, start listening to country music! You don't have to own a pickup truck in order to enjoy this genre. Country music endures because it speaks to the various human feelings and emotions we experience in everyday and not-so-everyday life. It can validate what we are feeling, and inspire us to push through to the other side of the situation.

"*Music is the shorthand of emotion.*"

—Leo Tolstoy

On the Flip Side

"MUSIC HAS CHARMS TO SOOTHE THE SAVAGE breast, to soften rocks, or bend the knotted oak," wrote William Congreve (1670 – 1729).

Those of us old enough to remember "45s" know that when you wanted to buy one song, you always got another one "on the flip side." Those smaller records (the vernacular now is "vinyl") would have a very popular song on the one side and a not as well-known song on the other side. As I recall, the one on the "flip side" did not usually have the same kind of message or even tempo. I guess it was a way of trying to give exposure to other artists and songs—or at least try to broaden the listener's musical horizons.

The flip side of energizing music is music to soothe the savage breast. Music that helps calm the spirit in the midst of raging emotions. Music that puts the trials and tribulations of the day "to bed" so we can sleep and get refreshed for another day!

For me, the "flip side" was a CD of ocean sounds. The waves crashing on shore…seagulls' plaintive cries…the bell clanging in a rocking buoy…a foghorn sounding an alarm…even the horn of a passing ship… and I am transported to a pleasant, warm sunny day at the beach on coastal Maine shores. And drift away I could…and would…. Like the tides that ebb and flow, so do our emotions. Good thing, too. We cannot always be fighting our way through to the other side of this dramatic shift in our lives; it takes too much energy! So, as we toss and turn to get our rest, we need to flip to our quieter selves and learn to relax. Music can help with that, too.

Music of nature—or Beethoven, or whatever soothes your soul—embrace it at the end of the day, that tomorrow might be faced with new courage and strength! Enjoy the flip side!

Just Skip It

HAVE YOU EVER HEARD SAD BANJO MUSIC? I COULD be wrong, but I think banjos were created to play upbeat, happy music. I even bought a secondhand banjo years ago because I loved having that music permeate my soul! (I later sold it to try to concentrate on my piping!)

Outward actions can change inward feelings.

In a "down" mood? I have just the prescription! Just skip it! Yes, go outside—or find a long hallway and just skip. You remember how, right? Keep skipping until you have a smile on your face. If you encounter others in your "journey," no doubt they will get a smile on their faces—after perhaps a quizzical look. Then keep skipping until you are laughing! Like banjo music, you can't skip and stay in a depressed mood; the two are incompatible!

Okay, are you back to reading now? Now that you had to stop and see if you really do remember how to skip?

We can learn a great deal by watching children at play. Left to their own devices, kids will run and jump and climb and explore and do all sorts of active, creative, and fun things. When did we stop doing these things? When did we succumb to the pressures to "act our age?"

Feeling down? Don't be concerned that others will think we have gone round the bend. Just skip it. You will feel better; I guarantee it!

Milestones and Millstones

HAVE YOU EVER SAT DOWN AND DRAWN A TIMEline of your life? By the time you reach your first birthday, several milestones have been reached: being born, rolling over, getting first tooth, sitting up, perhaps even taking first steps. As the years go by, more and more milestones are reached—and passed. That is one way we measure our lives, isn't it?

The term "milestone" comes from an actual stone that would be set in the ground next to a road to show how many miles it was to the next town. For weary travelers, it could be an encouraging sign that they were nearing their destination, having already covered a stretch of road. Encouraging signs are great things to have in our lives, aren't they?

In addition to the usual happy events and accomplishments, I would like to add "divorce" to the list of milestones.

So often, divorce has negative connotations. When you tell someone that you are divorced, the first reaction often is, "I'm sorry!" Divorce is too often seen as a millstone around one's neck, a burden that can weigh someone down and even prevent further growth and happiness.

It doesn't have to be! Why not designate divorce as just one more milestone in our lives? Seem odd? Well, maybe. But I think by designating it as such, we can change what might have been a millstone into a milestone and thus view life as full of new potential and possibilities. Divorce is just one more marker along life's journey! Let's get going!

Four-Fifths of the Way There

I WISH I HAD A DOLLAR FOR EVERY TIME SOMEONE has asked me how I'm doing, how it is going….

There are days when the most appropriate response would be, "I'm four-fifths of the way there!"

I am able to stand up, observe the weather, feed myself breakfast, answer texts…and then…I sit down in the living room. And that's about it; I just can't seem to rouse myself to do anything more. And where do I sit? My grandmother called it a "davenport." Some call it a "couch." I call it a "sofa."

And so how am I doing so far? I'm four-fifths of the way there.

I'll wait while you figure out the pun……….

Need help?

"S…that's one-fifth…O…that's two-fifths…F….that's three-fifths…A…that's four-fifths….

I hear you groaning now! But that's exactly how I get through some days: chuckling, using humor. Nothing profound, just taking it all one step at a time. Sometimes, just sitting on the sofa to see how I have done so far, and coming up with a plan to take it to the next step.

Four-fifths of the way there…. Now I will get up off the sofa, and do at least one positive thing today!

Never Forget

TODAY IS THE TWENTIETH ANNIVERSARY OF THE 9/11 attacks in my country. "Never Forget" seems to be a rallying cry, as if anyone twenty-five years of age and older could forget. We know where we were and what we were doing when we heard the news of the airplane crashes. Those of us who are sixty years old and older remember where we were and what we were doing when we heard of the assassination of our president, John F. Kennedy. Those even older than I, remember the attack on Pearl Harbor on December 7, 1941. We remember; we cannot forget.

Sometimes we wish we could forget—forget the negative things that have impacted our personal and communal lives. But we seem hardwired to remember.

Remember when you realized your marriage was beyond saving? Can you ever forget the feelings ranging from uncertainty about the future to the embarrassment of telling others of your divorce to the anger of wasted time (and other things) to the loneliness of facing an empty house?

No…we can't forget…but we must not wallow in these feelings either.

Thousands of innocent people suffer because of the unforeseen and uncontrollable actions of others, but to be dragged down into the mire of bitterness and hatred and assigning blame to others is not the path to wholeness.

The abundant life is available to all of us, if we will but acknowledge our need for help and accept it when it is offered.

"Those who wait for the Lord shall renew their strength."
- Isaiah 40:31

Unraveling the Past

THERE ARE SO MANY DETAILS INVOLVED IN A divorce, especially for a woman. A woman who added her husband's last name onto her own.

Take, for example, monograms. Yes, I know, it seems like a very small thing, but it is a "thing" nonetheless. As I am reclaiming my former, maiden name, I am shedding the last initial I had for forty-plus years. So when I looked at my luggage the other day, I decided to remove the stitching of that last initial.

As I wielded a seam ripper and scissors, I could not help but reflect on the memories of where my luggage and I had traveled and the space between trips. This time of contemplation helped me clear my mind—and my life—of the baggage of the past four decades. I must say it was very therapeutic!

However, when the initial was removed and my heart was feeling lighter, I realized the pinpricks of the stitching remained, no matter how hard I tried to close the miniature gaps in the fabric. Yeah, they will always be there.

You can unravel the past, but the past is still there. With Johnny Mercer, we can try to "accentuate the positive…eliminate the negative… latch on to the affirmative…" as far as that is possible.

I have found that by taking a notebook and writing down all the "red flags" I should have seen—and dealt with—helps me as I recount the past. Then I put that notebook away, those negative thoughts and memories slip back into the past, and I can move on.

A New Superpower!

WOW! I HAVE A NEW SUPERPOWER AND I DON'T even have to throw on a cape and squeeze into a pair of tights! Who knew?

What's my superpower, you ask? I am invisible! At least to some people, I am.

I had heard that when a couple splits up, the friends and acquaintances that they have in common have to choose sides. I have no trouble with that. Since the time word got out that we were going our separate ways, I discovered who my true friends are; and I really wasn't surprised who was there for me. What surprises me even now, though, is that those who did not "side" with me will not acknowledge my presence. I guess I must be invisible to them, for surely when our paths cross, common decency would mandate a small smile and a "hello." But there is no eye contact…no words of greeting. And I am not talking about relatives or even close friends. It is the reaction of a passing acquaintance, who, before this, would carry on polite conversation.

My wise father would say, "Consider the source." And I do. But I can't help but shake my head and wonder…what did I ever do to them?

My father would also say, "You should feel sorry for people like that." And I do, too. And I realize it is a waste of energy to spend any more time thinking about it all, so I wrap my cloak of invisibility that much tighter around me. I whisper a prayer of healing for all those who have eyes to see, but they see not, and for those of us who just wish to be seen and acknowledged. May all of us on this life's journey realize that we are beloved children of God—and everyone else is, too.

Exchanging Piece of Mind for Peace of Mind

"CAN YOU GIVE ME ONE GOOD REASON WHY I should not give him a piece of my mind???"

What might be meant as a rhetorical question really isn't a rhetorical question. I have an answer for that.

Giving someone a piece of your mind will rob you of peace of mind.

Has it ever been shown that giving someone a piece of your mind has improved a situation? Oh, yes, it might make you feel better in the short run to unload all those angry feelings onto the source of those feelings, but will the person change because you did? I doubt that.

Find someone—a trusted friend—who can stand beside you and absorb all those negative feelings without judgment. You need to choose a friend who will not judge you or the situation, someone who will not offer advice (that's not what you are looking for, is it???!!!), someone who will calmly be there for you and let you vent. Then rant and rant… until you have exhausted yourself and the situation.

Then take a good, long, brisk walk…or get on a stationary bike and pedal fast and hard…or hit a punching bag. Find a way to release all those pent-up feelings. It might take a while, but the process is important to see to its end.

Then, and only then, will peace of mind start to slowly creep in. That's the peace of mind you need in your life—not the other piece of mind. Your peace of mind is much more important—and lasting—and that will change things for you. No, it might not be the change you are looking for at first. But it is the one that will bring healing into your life. There is no substitute for that peace of mind.

Don't Fence Me In!

YEARS AGO I SPENT HOURS PUTTING IN A SPLIT rail fence alongside my garden. There was no gate; I just would step on the bottom rail and swing my leg over the top rail and jump in. This method had always worked. Then one day I stepped on the bottom rail and—crack!—it broke and there was no fixing it. So, I dug up the posts and removed what was remaining of the fence. And you know what? I like the openness and sense of "freedom" I feel every time I walk past the garden.

It wasn't until the fence was GONE that I realized that the fence wasn't serving any useful purpose (the neighbor's dogs I was trying to keep out had died years ago) and it actually was hindering some things. Some of the flowers were prevented from fully expanding and blooming. In the wintertime, the fence made it difficult to clear the walkway when it snowed. Carrying large packages in from my "visitor parking" had been made more difficult by its encroaching on the walkway width. Not only did I not need the fence, but removing the fence gave me a sense of freedom!

Limitations in our personal lives are often self-imposed. I started looking at things in my life that I had thought I couldn't do, or wouldn't do. And I started asking myself, "Why not?"

This is a brand new day! This is a brand new day for you, too. The possibilities are almost endless! Want to travel? Go ahead; you don't need a traveling companion. Want to go out to eat at a new restaurant? Why not? You can sit and dine and enjoy the experience. A new movie is in the theater? GO! What's stopping you? Only you. And the fence you have built of excuses. Here is the secret: no one else can even see the fence!

Mandated Etiquette

ON THE FIRST PAGE OF THE UNWRITTEN GUIDE, "What to Say to Children Who Are Having Disagreements" is emblazoned, "If you can't say something nice, don't say anything at all." How many times I heard that from my mom as I was growing up!!!

I think it must have been moms who wrote the rules for separation and divorce as spelled out in the lengthy legal agreements. Included in all of them (I am told) is: "Neither party shall make statements to each other, or to third persons, which are derogatory about the other party."

"But what if it is true?" I inquired of my attorney.

"You can roll your eyes," I was advised.

Sure sounds like, "If you can't say something nice, don't say anything at all."

Might be rather quiet...

Or your creative side might be commandeered: "Well, his socks always match."

What could possibly be gained by voicing the years of accumulated hurts? Once again, the wise words of my lawyer come to mind: "That's for you to tell your therapist; that's not what you are paying me for."

So find yourself a listening ear—hopefully one who won't charge an arm and a leg—so that you can pull yourself together with a smile on your face as you roll your eyes...and move on.

"And he has a nice selection of ties."

Mountains.......

A FRIEND OF MINE SHARED THIS: "THE MOUNTAIN you face now, someday will be far behind you…a distant memory. But the person you become will stay forever. And that was the reason for the mountain."

It has now been two years since he moved out. I am not the person I was two years ago. I'm not even the person I was a year ago. And that is a good thing.

I have examined my life…my priorities…and have searched for meaning and purpose. This is an ongoing process and I have to remind myself of that every now and then. Until the last breath that one takes, I think we are called to constantly be yielding our will and our carefully constructed plans to the Great Plan. I am not saying that this divorce— the mountain in my life—was in the Great Plan, but I am saying that it has helped shape me into the person I am today.

I hope others see changes. For example, I am a better friend, for others have extended their friendship to me and I have embraced those gestures and in turn, I try to reach out to others who may be going through difficult changes. My confidence in myself has returned. I see my faults and strengths and am working on being a better person. I am happier than I have been…perhaps ever!

I share these changes to show that there is a bright future waiting for each of us. Hang in there. Accept help. Reach out to others. Together we will get through this and be stronger on the other side of this mountain. Believe me. I've been there.

And Molehills....

HAVE YOU EVER SEEN A MOLEHILL? I DON'T THINK I have. I live where there are moles and voles and mice. I have seen where the ground is raised to show tunnels zigzagging underground. But actual molehills? I don't think I've seen any.

But those signs of tunnels underground have something to teach us as well.

There is always something going on below the surface of life. Sometimes we are made aware of the activity as things are raised where we can't help but see it. More often we don't even trip over these signs which are under our noses—and feet!

When our own lives are in upheaval, there are many around us whose lives are also in upheaval, but if we don't look beyond the end of our noses, so to speak, we will go on walking in our own little world, until and unless something trips us up—awakening us to those around us and the turmoil in their lives.

We need to get out of our "bubbles," and realize we are not alone.

The best way to help ourselves, sometimes, is to help others.

Mountains…molehills…underground tunnels…. There is no such thing as a level playing field. We just have to put one foot in front of the other and reach out a hand to our fellow travelers.

Getting to the Root of Things

THERE IS SOMETHING VERY SATISFYING ABOUT pulling up a weed by its roots. I rarely use gloves while working in the garden; I want to grab the offending plant and roots and soil in my bare hands and get the earth under my fingernails. It is a partnership I enjoy with my Creator.

If company is coming and I don't have much time to make my gardens look presentable, I am tempted to just trim off what shows above the ground…but I know that doesn't solve my weed invasion. It just puts off the inevitable; the offending plant will reappear, often in a matter of days!

No, we need to get to the root of things and rip them out, or we will never be able to sit back and enjoy the garden.

Whether we want to acknowledge it or not we have weeds in our lives. We need to really examine what is growing—and thriving—in the garden we call our lives. Are the various aspects of our lives beautiful and enriching to the eyes and hearts of the beholders? Or are nasty things creeping in and crowding out the beauty which could be there?

It is so much easier to blame others and ignore what we have done—or not done—which has resulted in the life we have now. We cannot undo the past, but the time is now to take stock in life and draw up a plan on how to improve it!

It is time to get the dirt under our fingernails. It is time to pull up those weeds, roots and all, so we can enjoy the gifts and attributes that have been planted in our hearts.

Old Book Sale

IT IS BITTERSWEET TO BROWSE THROUGH A BOOK sale, especially one that a library is holding. If there are really old books, you might even find the "due date" sheets in the back of the books; if they are really, really old, you might find people's names printed on those sheets. (I always loved to see who else might have read these treasures!)

I have been known to buy a few of these old "friends":

A book that a teacher read to the class, a chapter at a time, if we had finished our work for the day (*Mr. Popper's Penguins*).

The book that started my adventures in reading (from the Dick and Jane series—they are much maligned for their simplistic and repetitive nature, but they bring back fond memories…).

A book that I always hoped was based in historical fact (*Snow Treasure*).

A book that transports the reader to a special place and time (*The Secret Garden*).

I could go on and on….

Books are my friends, in so many ways, and it hurts to see them taken off the shelf and discarded. And I can relate in some ways. It is hard not to feel cast aside…to make room for someone or something else….

But like the old books that are put in the discard pile, we still have worth, even if it is not seen and recognized by the casual observer. Our stories have had their beginning and maybe even their "middle," but the end….

There are still adventures awaiting us, and for those willing to help us write the rest of our story!

Gold Stars

DO ELEMENTARY SCHOOL TEACHERS STILL PUT gold stars on the papers of students who get a 100 percent? I sure hope so! I loved seeing those stars on my papers; it gave me something to strive for each and every time.

But then there were the charts that had everyone's name on them—one for spelling and one for math. Every time someone got a 100 percent, a star would go up next to his or her name, and whoever got the line of stars to go all the way to the end got to take the chart home. I once had that "honor." I put the word "honor" in quotation marks because I threw it out as soon as I got home; I did not like seeing the names of my classmates who had received so few stars. I felt sorry for them; I'm sure they excelled at things in which I did not excel. (Sports is one example that springs to mind.) I did not mind competing against myself, so to speak, for those stars on my paper. I just did not want to even appear like I was competing against my peers.

Since my school days, some things have changed. Kids now get trophies for participation, rather than for being the best at something (especially sports). This practice has come under severe criticism; I daresay most likely it is from those whose trophies for excellence are still encircling their room (probably their den now?). I say, "Give all the kids trophies; why not? Does it really make them not strive for excellence?"

I still strive for excellence in my life, and try not to compare myself to others.

But I have to ask myself—and you—"How are things going today?" Well, we are here; we have made it this far and whether we realize it or not, we are doing quite well. Maybe we aren't 100 percent, but who is, really? I say, "Give yourself a gold star today!" You have earned it, just for striving to be the best you possibly can be.

A Cup of Love

EARLY ON IN THE SEPARATION/DIVORCE PROCESS a friend gave me a new mug. Now mugs I have aplenty, but this mug surpasses them all. It is the cup I now have my morning coffee in every day, because the message on the inside at the top, where I can see it with each sip, reads, "Always remember…you are loved."

As one is going through a breakup/shake-up, rejection can weigh heavily on the heart. But rejection by one is only that—rejection by one individual. All your friends, your true friends, are still there. They might not know what to say or do; it is an uncomfortable, scary territory for everybody. But they are there for you, perhaps even helping you take the first step toward healing with the simple, kind act of giving you a cup with a reminder for you to read each morning—you are loved.

And Hugs....

DOES YOUR COMMUNITY HAVE A "TOWN HUGGER?" Mine does! It is an official position designated years ago when a local man voiced his willingness to volunteer for this "job" he created. You can ask for a hug any time of day (or night, if you are reasonable about the hour) and H.S. will give you a bear hug, long enough to release some of the tension you are holding within. Many years later, after seeing the success of this job (and being reported in several articles around the state and the Northeast), another volunteer arose, saying that she was willing to be the female counterpart. Yes, I live in a unique and wonderful place in rural Vermont.

    Reminders of friends' love as you sip your coffee. Hugs to warm the soul. Signs of hope and healing are all around you, if you keep yourself open to discovering them. Take heart!

Ink Spots

SO... HERE IS MY FAVORITE CHILDREN'S MESSAGE:

Take a blank sheet of paper and hold it up for the kids (and adults) and ask them, "What do you see?" The answer, of course, is "a piece of paper." "Right!" Then take a black marker and in the middle of the paper, make a black spot about the size of the end of your little finger. Hold the paper up once more and ask, "Now what do you see?" "A black spot!" the children respond. "Yes...but what about the sheet of paper? Do you still see that?" About this time the kids think you are a little crazy...but continue. "Of course you do! But our eyes are drawn to the dot, aren't they? When sad or bad things happen to us, they are like the black spot on the paper—we focus on it and forget about everything else that is going on in our lives. But the good things are still there! There is more of the paper there that doesn't have a black spot on it! Let us try to see past the black dot and rejoice in the good that surrounds us each and every day."

Really this is a message for all of us, isn't it? We focus too much time and attention on the black ink spot that has come into our lives. It takes center stage. It is hard to see anything else going on in our lives. Each waking moment—and some of our dreams, our nightmares—seem consumed with our separation and divorce. We cannot escape it.

But there is so much more to us than this thing that has wormed its way (or thrust itself) into our lives. Look around! Take time to appreciate the rest of the sheet of paper on which our lives are written!

And then maybe someday we can take "white out" to that black spot and move on....

"Don't cling to a mistake just because you spent a lot of time making it."

—Anonymous

Trying to Remember

TALKING TO A FRIEND WHO WAS DIVORCED twenty years ago—after having been married for over ten years—she revealed to me that she couldn't recall a single happy memory of her time with her ex-husband.

So, I started to think…and I tried to remember happy times…or at least happier times…and realized I could relate to my friend's experience. Without getting into specifics, I could recall a few happy times…but each time a memory would surface, another aspect of the memory—a negative one—would also float to the top and overshadow the first.

But maybe there are no purely positive events in anyone's life. Is anything ever 100 percent super terrific? I think memory plays more of a role in our sense of happiness than we want to acknowledge. Memory can be a blessing and a curse.

I think the trick is to learn how to put those negative recollections and thoughts in a box, put the box on a very high shelf in one's memory bank, and resist the temptation to get out a "ladder" to pull down that box and revisit them.

So, is it that important to go back in time and relive days gone by? Do you really want to dredge up memories? Perhaps you do. But for me, I think I'll just choose to hold my loved ones close and try to forge new memories—happy ones—with them.

Yet...

MY FAVORITE WORD IN THE ENGLISH LANGUAGE consists of three letters: Y—E—T. It denotes a hope-filled future. Anything is possible! "I don't know Spanish…" YET! "I can't waterski…" YET! "I've never been to Peru…" YET!

What have you always wanted to do? What is holding you back? You still have time. You just need motivation, which can come in one little word: YET!

And closely tied to "yet" is the question: "What are you waiting for?"

When I reached one of my milestone birthdays, I decided that I was done waiting for someone to travel with me, or buy me that special "mother's ring," or go with me to events that I was interested in. What was I waiting for?

So I bought myself that mother's ring.
I camped (in a tent) on Prince Edward Island with one of my sisters.
I explored Acadia National Park with my other sister.
I bought that special pocketbook I always wanted.
I took bagpipe lessons.
I attended a play in a nearby town—two famous actors were playing the lead roles.
I joined in the yearly Scottish festivities in my state.
I took out my dusty skates and took to the ice. Not gracefully, but I tried!
I flew in a hot air balloon.
I was done waiting!

What haven't you done—YET—that you have a hankering to do? What are you waiting for? Encouragement? Go for it!

"What's Stopping You?"

CLOSELY TIED TO "YET" AND "WHAT ARE YOU WAITing for?" is "What's stopping you?"

The seeds of "yet" were planted in my youth. Unfortunately their growth was stunted somewhere along the way. But, I have to relate the groundbreaking "ceremony"….

When I was a junior in high school I was chosen to attend a leadership conference at a large university. Fortunately my two best friends were also chosen. In the evening, when others in our group decided to go to the movies, I told my friends, "We can do that at home. Let's explore the town!" (Today I don't think it would be considered wise for three teenage girls to wander that city, but this was in the 1970s.)

We found ourselves shopping in a large department store that had escalators. Offhandedly I remarked that I had always wanted to go up a "down" escalator. One of my friends said, "What's stopping you?" It was nearly closing time and there weren't many people around…so I took a running start and landed on the escalator and ran for all I was worth—and flew off at the top—as my friends stood at the bottom with their mouths hanging open. Then I turned around and hurled myself at the "up" escalator and, after some frantic moments, met my friends on the main floor. Now I am NOT recommending that anyone literally follow in my footsteps, but it was exhilarating! I had just crossed off one thing on my bucket list!

Looking back, I realize that sometime in the intervening years, something had imposed itself on me and I no longer listened to the urgings of my heart. I let something, or someone, or just the usual dictates of the "norm" stop me from launching into adventures.

No more! What's in store for me at my age now? I'm not sure.

Skydiving has also been on my list since my youth....

Out of Our Control

THERE ARE SO MANY THINGS THAT ARE OUT OF our control in this life.

For some of us, this concept is hard to grasp. There was a time when I was a preschooler and wanted to go outside to play, but it was raining. So I did what was logical to me: I asked my mom to make it stop raining. In later years my mom confided in me that it took her aback that I thought she had such power! But in my mind, I realized I didn't have control over the weather, but surely my mom did!

That marked the beginning of my disillusionment. There are some things that are out of my control, and even out of my mom's control!

Being separated, then divorced, to a large extent was out of my control. It isn't what I had planned—ever—but a marriage is a two-way covenant, a pact made by two people. If one person wants "out" of the relationship, there is nothing the other person can do.

That being said, I have to admit that there were things I could have done—or at least attempted—along the way to make the marriage "work," instead of hiding my head in the sand and plodding on with what was working in my life. I have to bear some of the responsibility for the failure of my marriage.

There, I said it. That was difficult for me to say. But now what? I felt like that little kid staring out the window, thwarted by things out of my control. I didn't like how it felt, but deep down I refused to accept the "role" of victim of my circumstances. I was determined to rise above, to find an alternative that I could live with. Like that little kid who could not play outside on the swing set, but played checkers inside instead, I was determined to enjoy the solitude my new circumstances brought me. I'm working on that…

But Not Out of Control...

THINGS HAD BEEN SET IN MOTION AND THEY were out of my control, but I was not out of control. Oh, yes, there was a time or two when I vented in a very loud voice to the four walls of my home. It was quite therapeutic at the time. But in general, I did not succumb to the negativity of the engulfing chaos.

Oh, the temptation was there, to be sure. But I found out how to handle these outbursts.

First of all, I reached out to friends who I knew would listen—not try to "fix" the situation. (I also had a friend or two who tried to pry out of me all the things that had gone wrong over the years—who thought I should try harder to keep the marriage together. Those "friends" I have since lost.)

One friend I've known since junior high and who is happily married affirmed me and encouraged me each step forward. Another friend is a widow, but is a great listener and instinctively knew when I needed to get out of Dodge and go thrift shopping or some other activity to take my mind off things. And, of course, I had my sisters who were definitely in my corner. But perhaps it was the friend who had also been recently blindsided by her husband of several decades who I needed to hear from most. The saying we have all heard is, "Misery loves company." The variation of that saying that rings even truer is, "Misery loves miserable company." Now she really understood where I was coming from.

All those things helped—and continue to help—but ultimately turning control over to God brought peace to my soul. I have to continue to remind myself to do that on a regular basis. As Victor Hugo said, "When you have accomplished your daily task, go to sleep in peace. God is awake."

A Cracked Pot

YOU KNOW THE STORY OF THE CRACKED POT?

In a land where one had to walk to the village well to get water, a man fashioned a wooden yoke to go around his neck with poles extending out on either side so that a clay pot could be attached on each end to hold water. One water jug was perfect; the other pot had a crack in it. Thus, when the man got home each day, one pot was full of water, while the other was only half full. Knowing this, the man planted seeds beside the path on the side of the cracked pot. In the spring, the man was rewarded with a blanket of gorgeous flowers on the side of the path where the cracked pot leaked the water from the well. The other side had only barren dirt.

Right now life might feel cracked—that those things that gave life meaning and purposes are trickling out. Life feels half full, if that. But maybe…those things are meant to go. Maybe those cracks are part of the plan to make life more beautiful.

Think about that for a minute….

None of us is perfect; we all have flaws in our personalities. But it is exactly those flaws, those imperfections that make us unique. It is those cracks that allow our true selves to shine through.

So embrace the fact that there are cracks in life, and you might be a "cracked pot." It is your eccentricities that make the world beautiful! How boring life would be if we were all perfect "pots."

Go scatter seeds of love along the pathways of your life. Watch them break open and blossom, watered with your tears and nourished and brightened by your smiles.

Sage Advice

NO MATTER WHERE WE ARE ON LIFE'S JOURNEY, aren't we always looking for advice? Advice from someone who knows what we are going through and can offer some good advice? Some sage advice?

As I was driving along one day, I was contemplating what wise advice I had received recently and what sage advice I could pass on to others in my situation. And then I started laughing out loud!

Sage advice....

Sage is not merely another word for "wise"; it is a plant, an herb. Now, I don't cook with many herbs (I'm of Scottish and English heritage) so I'm not going to give you a cooking lesson. But sage is also used in many cultures to help spirits move on to the next world. It is used to remove ghosts from haunted houses! People burn sage and, with a feather, let it waft into every crevice, encouraging spirits of the past to move on.

So why was I laughing? There are "ghosts" of my former life I need to have removed so their memory does not "haunt" me.

Here is my "sage" advice: Go through the rooms of your house, peeking into the corners and looking in the closets, and literally remove anything and everything that brings back memories you don't want to harbor in your next life, the new life you are creating for yourself. Leave only those things that put a smile on your face and love in your heart. The atmosphere in your house will feel lighter when these "ghosts" have been purged.

Feel free to share my "sage" advice!

Pruning for New Growth

RIGHT NOW IT IS THE DEAD OF WINTER, MY LEAST favorite time of year.

Driving along in my car just the other day, I was listening to a program on public radio about gardening. On this particular day, instead of talking about caring for house plants or selecting the best variety of tomatoes to order from seed catalogues, the topic was which trees and shrubs to prune in the winter. (Apple trees—yes! Lilac trees: no!)

The main lesson of the day was that if you trim off the top ("terminal") bud of an apple tree now, when the spring warmth arrives, the tree will shoot out branches from the bottom, enhancing the breadth of the tree.

I guess because of my father's biology background, my son's arborist studies, and my fascination with metaphors, I was captivated by the term "terminal bud." I'm sure I had heard that nomenclature before, but I suddenly stopped listening to the gardening program and started thinking about the pruning process that had begun in my life.

My life had been going onward and upward…or so I thought. But then, all of a sudden, the life I knew was "nipped in the bud." There would be no more upward growth. Or so it seemed. Then the new growth appeared! Opportunities opened up for me that wouldn't have ever happened in my "old" life. I truly began "branching out!" I landed an interim position that affirmed my professional talents. I discovered new strengths. I formed new friendships. None of these things would have been possible in my old life. The former things had to be pruned away in order for new growth to sprout out from the base. Like the pruning of trees, our lives need to be pruned of dead wood on a regular basis.

New life is waiting for us—get pruning!

Waves

DIVORCE HAS BEEN LIKENED TO DEATH—DEATH of a marriage—and the ensuing emotions can sometimes be likened to grief. It is a process of learning to accept what has happened and looking for a way forward. There are good days and bad days. There may be stretches of weeks where life is moving along and then there are times when things seem stalled and perhaps even scary. I know it has been so for me. Just when I think I have a handle on things, something pops into my mind and I suddenly find myself in a funk. Grief is like waves washing ashore: sometimes like gentle waves lapping at one's feet, sometimes like a tsunami, knocking one down and trying to drag its captive out to sea.

For each of us it is different, for we are different, and our circumstances are different.

Talking with a friend recently I told her that I had been doing fine… then a stranger, helping me fill out a basic form, asked me my marital status. "Divorced." The word just seemed to hang in the air…and a wave came at me full force. She probed: was I grieving the death of my marriage as it had been, or was I grieving over the marriage I had hoped and planned for?

That rhetorical question abruptly stopped the wave. As it ebbed away, I realized I was smiling at the wisdom revealed in her words. My life hadn't been what I had hoped for…a long time. The grief process had started long ago, but it had been an undercurrent that I could not or would not acknowledge. I'd been afraid of being dragged by the rip current into waters way over my head and wasn't sure I could swim long enough and hard enough to find my footing.

But I am on the beach now, watching the flotsam of the past float away.... My eyes are on the horizon, looking with hopeful anticipation toward the future.

Card-Carrying?

IN OUR WALLETS AND PURSES WE CARRY MANY cards—for identification, for paying bills, taking out a book in the library, for health insurance, and on the list goes....

After receiving the official divorce decree, complete with the judge's signature and court seal, I found that I needed that slip of paper—for updating my driver's license, changing my name on bank accounts, for opening a new credit card, and on the list goes....

So I started carrying it with me at all times in my pocketbook. I found that seeing it in my purse, even when I didn't need to show my "new" identity, was somehow comforting and even affirming. It was a visible sign of the new life on which I was embarking; it signaled the start of things to come! It was as if it were the springboard into the unknown…but it was okay. I could begin to reinvent myself. That paper gave me permission for new adventures. What might have been depressing for others, actually gave me a sense of empowerment. It felt like a passport to a new land.

When I told a friend what I was carrying in my pocketbook, she replied that one day I wouldn't need to carry it around anymore. One day I would be comfortable enough to leave it at home, merely filing it among my other papers, so I would know where it was if and/or when I need it. I would feel empowered enough that I wouldn't have to have it close at hand.

That day has come.
Alleluia!

Calculus—and More!

IF YOU LIKE PUZZLES, CHANCES ARE YOU LIKE math, and vice versa.

I have always loved puzzles of many kinds, shapes, and sizes. I have also loved math, especially algebra. In school I took algebra in eighth grade, geometry in ninth grade, trigonometry in tenth grade, and "Math 12" (which was basically pre-calculus) in eleventh grade. So I naturally signed up for Advanced Placement Math my senior year—calculus.

Now I don't know if I was suffering from senioritis, but the appeal of math dwindled more and more as I sat in that class. Then one day I had an epiphany. In an instant I saw calculus as it was for me: a waste of time.

The math problem of the day involved a bathtub. The time of the day was given to us. The dimensions of the bathtub were given to us, even the curvature of the sides. We were told that the water faucet was turned on and was flowing into the tub at a designated rate per minute. At what time, they wanted to know, would the bathtub overflow?

Why figure out when it would overflow??? JUST PULL THE PLUG!

I really couldn't have cared less about that bathtub and the inevitable water all over that bathroom floor. For the rest of the school year I went through the motions of doing the calculus problems, but my heart wasn't in it. Where was my joy of learning math? It had gone down the drain the day of the "bathtub incident." Unfortunately, I didn't leave that math class at the same time. I stuck it out until June.

As I reflect on my marriage, I realize that there had been several "bathtub incidents" over the course of those four decades, but I stuck it out. The joy had gone down the drain, but I remained. I sometimes wish I had had the courage to pull the plug and reclaim my joy.

Dreaded Day?

WHETHER SINGLE BY CHOICE OR BY CIRCUMstance, there is one day every year that the "unattached" dread:

Valentine's Day.

On calendars, people draw a heart around the fourteenth of February. Commercials on TV suggest that flowers, chocolates, even expensive jewelry are the way to show true love on this special day of celebration. But if you don't have that "someone," it is a day to dread, to be sure.

This year I had even more reason to dread the day. I was in a hospital two hours away from home, awaiting eye surgery. People were coming and going, all asking different, yet pertinent questions about my health history. As I waited for the anesthesiology team to arrive, one nurse and I chatted about the significance of the day—and discovered our mutual love of dark chocolate.

Surgery went according to plan and an hour and a half later I was in post-op, lying prone, as was necessary. I heard footsteps approach and then stop. The nurse on duty spoke to the new arrival. "She's awake. You can give those to her." Since I wasn't allowed to raise my head, I couldn't see her, but I recognized her voice—it was the pre-op nurse! She had come to see me; she brought me two Godiva dark chocolate hearts!

Who said Valentine's Day was just for "lovers?" It is for friends, relatives, and occasionally for strangers who meet in unlikely places, who share a moment in time and a love for dark chocolate.

The world is full of caring, considerate people. If you keep your heart open, there's nothing to dread about Valentine's Day!

Stick a Pin in It!

THERE ARE MANY EXPRESSIONS WHOSE MEANING escapes me. The latest one is: "Stick a pin in it!"

I asked a few friends what it meant, especially in relation to divorce, for I had been advised to "stick a pin in it." I received three different interpretations.

The first said it was a World War II reference to a hand grenade. To stick a pin in a grenade is to render it "safe." So the analogy of sticking a pin in a situation is to do what is necessary to prevent everything from exploding in your face. Your actions might not render the actions of others as totally harmless, but you make sure your actions don't make it any worse. In other words, take the situation as it is and try not to let it get out of hand.

The second replied that it means to mark that chapter of life as "done," and move on. You have come to a "full stop" like they say in the UK (their word for a period at the end of a sentence). We have come this far—don't look back. Turn the page and see where the story goes!

The third commented (tongue in cheek, I'm sure—not trying to be offensive to anyone's beliefs or culture) that it was a reference to a voodoo doll—and seeking vengeance! Stick a pin in it—you'll feel better! Seek a little vengeance, albeit on an inanimate object.

Of these three, I choose to adopt the first two. Either of these will lead to healing. The third, though humorous at first, only fosters negative emotions.

We are better than that.

Let's stick a pin in the situation and move on with our lives!

I Am Enough...Not!

HAVING TAKEN OFF MY ENGAGEMENT RING...AND then my wedding band...I felt bereft. After four decades of wearing those rings, I found myself feeling for them, and even looking at my hand. I really missed having something there. I had other rings, but they weren't everyday rings. So I started a search online for some kind of replacement. I soon happened upon a ring with a saying on it, but I hesitated. Was that really what I wanted? Then one day with a simple click of the mouse, the ring was on its way.

I still wasn't sure if it was the ring I wanted, even after it arrived a few days later, but I put it on, and read the inscription. I continued to read it every so often throughout the day. But it still didn't feel quite right. In fact, it felt a bit blasphemous. So a few days later when I was walking the dog and it slipped off my finger and fell among the leaves on the path, I realized I felt a little relieved. But considering my heritage (Scottish), I didn't want it to go to waste, so I looked down, and sure enough it was there. I picked it up and placed it back on my finger. When I lost it the second time (somewhere in the house I think), I didn't try too hard to find it. I still haven't come across it—it has been over a year and a half.

What did the ring have written on it?

"I am enough."

But I'm not.

When I first bought it, it was saying—to me—that I didn't need a man to "complete" my life. But as the days went by, it took on a hubristic feeling, as if I were saying I don't need anyone else! But I do. I need my friends, and most of all I need God.

If I ever find that ring, I'm getting rid of it.

Symbols

SO...I STILL DIDN'T HAVE AN EVERYDAY RING FOR my left hand. I had a pinkie ring I had made especially for me with my sons' birthstones. I had my grandmother's five-pearl ring. I had the ring my mom had when she was in high school. I even had a ring I bought myself with a piece of green glass in it to represent my birthstone (an emerald; the real things are too costly for me to buy); but when I wear it, it fits on my right hand. I needed something on my left hand. So, I went back to the internet.

I wanted my new ring to embody my new life going forward. I needed a new symbol, a positive symbol of life and growth. That's when I stumbled upon the tree of life.

This symbol was not new to me. I own an apron with the tree embroidered on it (though the times I remember to wear an apron when I'm in the kitchen are few and far between). Over my sink, I have a plaque with the "I" of "faith" replaced with a tree. I had replaced the sign over my door with my "recovered" last name spelled out in metal amid the tree of life. And since I live in the woods, a tree of life ring seemed most appropriate. So I ordered this ring, as a pinkie ring for my left hand. It was the appropriate symbol of new life I had been searching for.

Rooted in love—from family and friends.
Growing upwards in the light of the Son.
Branching out into a new life of possibilities.
May you find a symbol of the new life—and growth—that awaits you!

A Little Nutty

"Dreams are like acorns; tended carefully they come true. Never forget just like the acorn, there's great power in you!"
—A. S. Waldrop

ONE DAY, A FRIEND HANDED ME A SMALL BOX AND inside it was that poem and a glass acorn. I joked with her that she was calling me a little "nutty!" I have kept that poem and that acorn on the table in my breakfast nook where I see it every morning.

I have always been attracted to acorns. I'm not exactly sure why, but even today, I bend down and pick up acorns when I walk through the woods. Maybe it is because I realize the power that I hold in my hand—the power to become a mighty oak tree.

But not all acorns become oak trees. Some are eaten by squirrels and other wildlife. Some are picked up and put on a shelf. Some just fall in inhospitable places where the acorn just can't sprout and grow. Some start off embedded in the ground and growing, but something or someone impedes its growth, perhaps even kills it wittingly or unwittingly.

But even if it lands in fertile soil and gets all the water and sun and nourishment it needs to thrive, it doesn't just grow and grow and grow; there are times when it doesn't grow at all. In the winter it rests and waits for the warmth of the earth to return.

Like the acorn, there is great power in each of us. There are still dreams that seek to come to fruition in your life. These dreams need to be recognized and fed and nurtured. However, there will also be times of much needed rest. If your dreams seem to be at a standstill, perhaps they are just resting. Be patient. They will be realized!

Oh, and guess what? When I am looking for new furniture, I gravitate toward…....OAK!

Lists

THERE ARE PEOPLE WHO GO THROUGH LIFE WITHout making lists, I'm sure. I'm not one of them. I have the usual grocery shopping lists, lists of projects that need to be done (I have short-range and long-range lists of those!), lists of people to send Christmas cards to (though I haven't done that for the past few years), lists of activities to do every day (exercise, read, practice my bagpipes, etc.), and, of course, my bucket list.

There is great satisfaction I find, in being able to cross things off my lists.

However, I know one person who does things a little differently. She starts off the day with a blank sheet of paper. She places it on her dining room table and places a pen beside it. When she accomplishes a task, she walks over to the piece of paper, writes down the task, and then promptly draws a line through it. That way, she says, at the end of the day, she can look back and see all the things she has done, feeling good about the day! Therefore, there is, she claims, no guilt of leaving things undone at the end of the day.

Well, maybe she has a point. But she has unfinished tasks; she just chooses not to have them written down and staring her in the face!

Lists are tools we can use to help us handle the challenges and demands that life puts upon us. The new status of separated/divorced probably will have you adding new roles and responsibilities to your daily/weekly/yearly lists of chores. The key, I think, whether you write "to-do" lists or "done" lists, is not to be overwhelmed. Lists can help us organize and put things into perspective. Lists help us prioritize how we use the gift of time.

We each have twenty-four hours in every day. How will we use this gift?

Yes, You Can

IN ANY RELATIONSHIP, BE IT AT WORK OR AT HOME or in social situations, there is a division of responsibilities. Sometimes this delineation is the result of careful planning and negotiation, but more often it seems to be the result of natural inclination. For example, I am a vegetarian. Since I do not eat meat, I do not cook meat (at the request and urging of the meat eaters in my family). Therefore, I do not grill. I have said for years that I don't even know how to turn on the grill. If I learned how, I reasoned to myself, it would become my job. (When I "learned" how to start the lawnmower and the weed whacker, those chores did become mine!)

In this new life, however, nothing is off limits. I have to "learn" how to do it all, or hire someone to do it for me, or rely on my sons and friends to lend me their expertise (and teach me along the way!). I have been very fortunate in that regard.

A friend of mine, who is also divorced after decades of marriage, excitedly told me this winter that when her snowblower quit working, she fixed it! I shared in her enthusiasm!

I find that the biggest stumbling block to getting things accomplished around my house…is me. I put things off, questioning my abilities. Can I really put up tiling backsplash? Can I lay down pavers for a walkway? The hardest part of any project is starting, believing that you can do it. Don't we all need a shot of confidence?

So, I officially give you that confidence.

I believe in you!

You can do it!

Go for it!
And you will be amazed at what you can do.

A New Coat

THERE IS SOMETHING ABOUT A FRESH COAT OF paint, isn't there? Or at least there is for me.

Slowly, but surely, I have been painting the walls of my house, one room at a time. I chose a new color—a soft, warm hue. I needed something new and different. And when a room is completed, I like to just stand and gaze and marvel at how the room has been transformed.

That being said, I have to confess that I really do not enjoy the painting process. There is a lot of work that goes into preparing the room to be painted, from moving furniture to spackling the unnecessary holes in the walls to taping the areas that should not be painted (think woodwork and windowpanes). It is very time consuming just doing all that. Then when I do get to start wielding a brush and roller, it seems like I end up with a quarter of the gallon of paint on me and my clothes—sometimes even the dog!

But when a wall or a closet of a room in completed, there is something very pleasing about that new coat of paint. It covers imperfections in the wall. It glosses over the mistakes and bumps and scratches that have occurred since last it was painted. It gives off a sense of accomplishment—a new start!

So, what if you don't need to paint your house/apartment? May I suggest a new coat anyway? Grab an L.L. Bean or Land's End catalogue and order one! Yes, a new coat or jacket can often achieve the same purpose—to lift your spirits and acknowledge a new beginning. Even though I was in the painting project mode, I also bought a new jacket…

and turtlenecks…even a new dress. This is not an either/or choice. Do what feels right!

So every time I gaze at my light green walls or slip on my new clothes, I smile, because I am being reminded that this is my new life and I am comfortable in it.

Don't Go There

SOMETIMES AT NIGHT THE TRAIN OF MY RANDOM thoughts gets on the wrong track. "Coulda, shoulda, woulda… coulda, shoulda, woulda… coulda, shoulda, woulda…"

We all know that train is going nowhere. It might go around and around the mountain of regrets, but it always ends up at the depot for more refueling…then just goes round and round and round again. "Coulda, shoulda, woulda… coulda, shoulda, woulda… coulda, shoulda, woulda…"

Revisiting the past can help us see the mistakes and poor choices we made—we have all made them—but there is a limit to how much time we should spend there. What should we have done ten…twenty years ago? How would life be different if we had done things differently? We will never really know for sure, will we? And such trips down those tracks certainly don't lead us to a good place. We can only arrive at the land of discontent and wishful thinking. Don't go there!

The past is not where we are headed.

We need to board the outbound train of future possibilities. Let's take the lessons we have learned along the way and head out!

Do you hear the whistle of the train? It is leaving the station! Where is it going? We aren't sure…the future can be scary.… But the train conductor yells to us, "All aboard!" holding the ticket to our future.

Let's climb aboard and hold on tight for the ride of our lives.

OCD.... or CDO....or COD

FIRST AND FOREMOST, LET ME SAY THAT I AM NOT a clinician. Also let me express my apologies to anyone who has been diagnosed with OCD (Obsessive Compulsive Disorder). That being said, I believe I have a touch of OCD, or like I like to say, "CDO"—I like things in alphabetical order!

I grew up with the saying, "A place for everything and everything in its place." I took that to heart. For example, as a child, one of my sisters washed the dishes, the other sister dried the dishes, and I put them away. We had dishes that came in four colors: pink, blue, yellow, and gray. There were two of each color in each size. I HAD to have them in the cupboard in that order: two pink on top, then the two blue, then the two yellow, and then the two gray. If someone else happened to put dishes away and didn't follow that order, I would go in the cabinet and change them! And this was at a relatively young age! My mom made a comment that I was being a bit rigid in this endeavor, but it didn't change my love of order, or my obsessiveness in keeping at least the dishes in order.

This has expanded through the years to my trying to have my "life" be in order....

The separation and divorce threw a monkey wrench into that! So I changed the initials once again, this time to COD—not "Cash On Delivery," but rather "Confidence in One's Dreams." I now realize that control really is an illusion. So let's put aside our expectations and plans, and imagine the possibilities for a new life! Has something or someone been holding you back from a dream or goal you once had?

Expand your horizons! Step into the unknown with confidence! What lies ahead? I'm not sure, but I'm taking the reins and am Creating my Own Destiny!

    You can, too!

Personal Growth

WHEN I WENT FOR MY DRIVER'S LICENSE AT THE age of seventeen, the DMV asked how tall I was. Proudly, I stood up as tall as I could and announced, "Five feet, one and a half inches." The official told me, "We don't deal with fractions; I will put five feet, two inches." "Let's be honest," I replied. "I'm closer to five foot one than five foot two."

Then, about seven years ago, when I went for my annual check-up at the doctor's office, a new nurse was measuring me and declared that I was five feet, one and three-quarters. "That can't be!" I responded. "Honey," she said rather condescendingly, "we all shrink as we get older." "No, you don't understand," I smiled. "I've never been five feet one and three-quarters in my life! I've been five feet and one and a half inches—and I have had to stretch to get that!"

Fast forward to my last physical. I was measured once again. This time I was declared five foot two!!!!!

When the doctor appeared in the exam room, I proudly proclaimed that I was growing! (I'm in my sixties!) Her response? "Now that a weight has been lifted off your shoulders, maybe you are standing taller! Perhaps a study should be done on divorced women to see if they are 'growing!'"

When you are vertically challenged, every quarter of an inch is monumental! But even more monumental is the personal growth that goes on inside you. Yes, I have been growing and finding new talents, abilities, and ways to express my creativity. My contentment in life—and of life—has grown in ways I could not have anticipated a few years ago, much like I didn't expect to "grow" to five foot two in this lifetime!

GROWTH! It is always possible—in surprising ways!

Food for Thought

FOOD IS MORE THAN JUST EATING CALORIES TO fuel the body.

For example, what food from your childhood brings back fond memories of the warmth of a kitchen after a day of sledding…or time spent with loved ones around a table…or a grandmother's favorite recipe? Conversely, what food did you detest growing up that you haven't touched since you left your parents' home?

Looking back since the separation/divorce, I realize that there are foods that I haven't eaten since he moved out! I couldn't have told you before that time that I really didn't care for them, but I realize now that I ate some food because the other person in the house liked it! Now I eat only what is pleasing to my palate—and doesn't bring up unpleasant memories. I also have been experimenting with unusual foods and new recipes!

As food feeds the body, new ideas and experiences feed the soul.

I have started "listening" when a fresh idea pops into my mind. Where did it come from? Is it something to explore? Someone recommends a book and I make the time to read it. I think of someone I haven't consciously thought of in ages; I try to reach out to say "hi." Someone mentions an activity or hobby that I have "always" wanted to do; I put aside a few minutes each day to explore it. An opportunity arises to visit a new place; I make every effort to go! It is the little things that collectively make up the joy in one's soul.

It is as important to feed the soul as it is to feed the body. An undernourished soul is as sad a sight as an undernourished body.

So go, have that hot fudge sundae—with a side of dance lessons!

The Key

IT GOES WITHOUT SAYING THAT RELATIONSHIPS are complex, almost living organisms.

In the movie, *A Muppet Christmas Carol*, Ebenezer Scrooge's young love and one-time fiancée, Belle, sings a song entitled, "The Love Is Gone," when she breaks their engagement. More than love, I believe the respect was gone. Often you can't point to one incident or a specific day and time when the respect disappeared. More often, respect erodes little by little until one day you realize it's gone. And once it is gone, I honestly don't know how you can bring it back. A lost love might be rekindled, but a loss of respect? That just seems permanent, spurring a person to acknowledge that and move on.

While reading through posts on Facebook, I sometimes come across posts from friends I don't agree with. I can live with that. But then there are the times that I find a post offensive and unkind. That is when I go to their page and unfriend them. I have lost respect for them.

The last time I unfriended someone, a light bulb went off in my brain. I can disagree with someone, but when I lose respect for them, the relationship is over.

So I think the key to a healthy relationship—be it friendship or marriage or whatever!—is respect. When you lose respect for the other person, I don't see how a future is possible between you. And when you move on, take with you this key: Honest respect for another can carry you through rough patches and even great storms in life. But without it, the relationship is already gone. Nothing can bring it back.

So, how do I end on a positive note? Well, there are people out there who are worthy of your respect, and plenty of people you already respect. Key in on those relationships and build stronger ties with them.

Alone Does Not Have to Mean Lonely

YESTERDAY WAS NATIONAL DOG DAY. (WHO COMES up with these things?) As far as I can tell, all that means is that you are supposed to post a picture of your dog on Facebook. So, less than fourteen hours ago, I found a picture of me and my dog and posted it. My hair was shaggy (past due for a haircut) and the dog wasn't looking in the direction of the camera, but hey; it fit the bill.

As of this moment, seventy-six of my friends like my post and of those, twenty-seven people took the time to type in a comment. That means that seventy-six people in this world thought of me in the last day. I might further hazard a guess that others who aren't on Facebook and therefore didn't see the picture, nevertheless might have thought of me for one reason or another. That makes me smile. I realize that I'm part (albeit, perhaps, a small part) of their lives.

I live alone now. It is part of who I am. But just because I am alone, doesn't mean I have to be lonely. And, in turn, I am reminded that clicking a "like" or a "care" on others' posts lets them know I am thinking of them. Despite what others may think or say about Facebook, personally I thank Mr. Zuckerberg for creating this tool to connect people far and wide.

Oh! It's up to seventy-eight "likes" and twenty-seven comments! Now seventy-*nine* "likes"....

Eighty-two....

Eighty-four....
I might be alone, but I needn't feel lonely.

Labels

EVER SINCE I WAS A LITTLE GIRL, I HATED LABELS. To be more specific, "tags." The tags at the back of dresses and T-shirts would be ripped out, because they "itched" me. My mom would try to intercept before I ripped so hard that a hole in the fabric would appear! No one was happier when manufacturers decided to make tagless articles of clothing!

In another vein of thought, I don't like the labels we so often and thoughtlessly place on people who do not think or look like we do. I don't like the labels people put on me!

Sometimes the labels *are* accurate…but still, I don't like them. Labels create divisions—us and them—and it is hard to cross these chasms once they are formed.

"What is your marital status?"

Why do they need to know? Most of those forms that ask that question really don't need to know.

I remember the first time I was confronted with that question. I marked the "divorced" box, but it just didn't feel "right." I was divorced all right, but why slap that label on myself?

Soon thereafter, I was talking with a girlfriend of mine, sharing my most recent "labeling" experience. She could relate! She marks the "single" box. I think I will too, from now on.

I suppose there will always be labels, but I, for one, am now consciously trying to avoid labeling people different from myself, in the hopes that it might catch on in some small way, "and the world will live as one." (John Lennon)

Laughter Crowds out Pain and Anger

A FRIEND OF MINE SHARED THIS THOUGHT: "ONE cannot hold both pain and laughter at the same time." To take this a step further, it isn't possible to hold anger and laughter at the same time, either.

Laughter is unique to us human beings. (Hyenas really don't "laugh"—we interpret their vocalizations as sounding like laughter; they aren't sharing a joke.) Laughter is our release valve. Perhaps other animals don't require such a thing. But laughter is a gift we give ourselves when we allow humor into our lives.

But at times like these, it is often easier to be sullen, angry, depressed... anything but in the mood to laugh. But it is exactly what we need to do.

I have found that the easiest way to laugh these days is to take the advice found in the musical, *Singing in the Rain*. In that musical Donald O' Connor sings: "Make 'em laugh, make 'em laugh; don't you know everyone wants to laugh?"

So every day I try to make someone laugh. As they are laughing, I laugh, too.

Example? For the first time in my life, I had to have a root canal. (They really aren't as bad as many try to make them out to be.) Then, of course, I had to come back several weeks later to have the permanent crown cemented in. Before I left home that morning, I opened the toy chest that contains dress-up clothes I have accumulated over the years, and pulled out part of a costume. As I was sitting in the chair waiting for the dentist to enter the room, I slipped it out of my pocketbook and placed the bejeweled crown on my head. Yes, it brought about smiles, chuckles, and laughs from everyone in the dentist's office.

Laughter truly is the best medicine—to help heal broken bones and broken hearts.

Celebration!

PEOPLE'S REACTIONS TO HEARING OF MY DIVORCE have been quite varied. As I noted earlier, one of the first people I told laughed! (She didn't think I was serious.) Most people say something like, "I'm sorry." Well, how does one respond to that? I smile wanly. I had heard that word before, and knew the definition (in a way that shows no energy or enthusiasm) but had never experienced it in my own life.

But then one day after my usual dialogue about my separation/divorce, the woman looked me straight in the eye and asked, "How do you feel?" Without even taking a split second to consider how to respond, I announced to her and anyone within hearing distance, "LIBERATED!"

At first I was a taken aback by my response and then realized I was no longer smiling wanly. I was smiling broadly, and yes, with enthusiasm!

It was one of my first steps to embracing my new life. Oh, I've had many a step back and forth since then, but it felt good to acknowledge this freeing feeling.

This woman then went on to say how a woman in a similar situation had thrown a party. I didn't do that. And another woman had gone through her house "smudging" to get rid of negative feelings and old "ghosts." I didn't do that either.

But I did allow myself to feel a sense of relief wash over me.

I let go of the past—and what might have been—and took a step, albeit shaky at first, into the future. My future.

Let the celebration begin!

Braking for the Future

WHEN A FRIEND ASKED ME WHAT HAPPENED TO my marriage, I realized I could point to a lot of "little" things that had happened over the course of four decades. So, my friend responded, "It's like the brakes on a car. Over time and the many miles one puts on a car, the brakes are worn down little by little, without you even being aware of the wearing away, and if you aren't careful, one day you go to step on the brakes and there is nothing left to stop the car!"

Fortunately, most of us have our cars inspected and maintained on a regular basis, so those disasters don't befall us. But how many of us check the status of our relationships on a similarly regular basis? I know I didn't. Not really.

And now my brakes are shot.

The rotors, too.

And here the analogy ends. Unlike cars, relationships don't have spare parts just waiting to be installed. If one part of the relationship doesn't want to fix the "vehicle," the whole thing just gets sent to the junkyard…and the crusher.

If there is any good news that can come out of it all, perhaps lessons have been learned.

I know that with my car, it only took having to replace the rotors once to make me see to it that my brakes are up to code. It was an expensive lesson, but a lesson that engrained in me good vehicle maintenance!

As anyone knows, divorce is expensive, but maybe if there is a next time, the little things will be dealt with before they become insurmountable.

Here's hoping…

Ready...? Or Not...?

AS I WRITE THIS, IT'S BEEN OVER TWO AND A HALF YEARS since the separation and over a year and a half since the divorce became final. I think I've been adjusting well. In fact I recently had told a friend who had been offering to find a man for me to date that I thought I was ready to try. Before he even had time to think about it, out of the blue a man who is a widower asked if I'd like to go out to lunch with him. "Sure!" I responded without another thought. Frankly, I was flattered.

Another friend who has kept me buoyed up throughout the past few years, asked me, "Are you ready?" "Yeah, I'm ready to move ahead," I told him. Then my mind went to work. Was I really ready? It literally had been decades since I had been on a date. "It's only lunch!" I retorted in the tangled web of my brain. But…the doubts crept in more and more as the days passed.

When a pastor leaves a congregation, the general rule is that between "settled" pastors, there should be an interim pastor who is there one month for every year the previous pastor served that particular church.

Perhaps the same time frame should be used in divorced/widowed situations. And maybe the interim period should be filled with friends and platonic "safe" relationships. I know a few couples who have jumped into marriage within a year of losing a spouse one way or another, and have lived to regret it. The "work" of healing had not been completed and the new relationship suffered for it.

Maybe I'm ready….
Maybe I'm not….
Time will tell.

Stage Production

"ALL THE WORLD'S A STAGE, AND ALL THE MEN AND women merely players; they have their exits and their entrances…"

Enter stage right….

I am not the first (obviously) who has come to see life as a play we are cast in, or cajoled to play, or even pushed into. For a moment I would like to think about the other players on the stage we call our life.

As I look back over the years, I see people come into my life for a time…then leave. Why did they come into my life at that particular time? And why did they leave? I think it is because we all are on this earth to learn from others, and help others to learn from us, how to live and love and do so abundantly. Perhaps a person came into our lives to teach us something; perhaps they came because they needed to learn something from us. And when they left, maybe it was because they had learned their lesson…or we had learned what we needed from them…or maybe they were yanked offstage because their performance was just so bad that the stage manager had to give them the hook!

Does the audience miss the actor's role? I doubt it. They are caught up in the storyline! As the main character in our play, we, too, shouldn't grieve (at least not for long) the movement of the play, for the PLAYWRIGHT has the actor's best interests at heart. Let's ride this out and see where it goes! People enter our lives…and exit our lives…and our plotlines are intertwined with others…and despite what the critics in the audience might say, we are doing a fine job!

Now…onto the next act!

Seeking...

SO I AWOKE THIS MORNING ABOUT AS GRAY AND overcast as the day. It took several attempts by the dog to rouse me out of bed. I hadn't slept well. I just wanted to pull the covers over my head…but my thoughts started swirling in my brain and I couldn't turn them off. As I reached for the clothes I had worn yesterday (it was easier than trying to think of what else I might wear today), this quote popped into my consciousness:

> "Seek peace and pursue it."
> —Psalm 34:14

Memorizing scripture has never been easy for me—I haven't seen it as a priority in my life—so when something comes to me seemingly out of the blue, I have to pay attention to it.

What had I been pursuing? It certainly wasn't peace.

What did I crave more than anything in my life?

And Persuing...

HOW HAD I BEEN TRYING TO FIND IT? I HAD stripped away a lot of my possessions (less is more). I had given my house a facelift (covering up the old life). I had organized closets and shelves. I had gone out of my comfort zone and tried a new hobby (contra dancing). I tried meeting new people. Even writing these essays has been an attempt to find peace.

But my mistake was trying to find peace. It's not like the dime I discovered on my morning walk. Peace does not lie in my actions or reactions. Peace is not just waiting for me to discover it. Peace lies within.

Easier said than done. But today I will try to quiet my thoughts so my soul might at least glimpse peace.

Seek peace and pursue it.

On and On and On and On....

I STILL HAVE A SMALL STACK OF INDEX CARDS with ideas written on them for more essays:

Sometimes Quitting Is for Winners

or

When Losses Aren't Losses
Exhale the Past, Inhale the Future
Accepting Help
Tohubohu*

By now, though, I think that YOU could write an essay just as well, if not better than I could. If so, I have accomplished my mission: to bring hope and healing to others who may find themselves in this rocking boat of separation and divorce. I only ask that you share your insights with others, that peace may spread.

That said, let me share one more thought by C. JoyBell C. before my benediction:

"I have come to accept the feeling of not knowing where I am going. And I have trained myself to love it. Because it is only when we are suspended in midair with no landing in sight, that we force our wings to unravel and alas, begin our flight. And as we fly, we still may not know where we are going to. But the miracle is in the unfolding of wings.

You may not know where you are going, but you know that as long as you spread your wings, the wind will carry you."

*Tohubohu =a state of chaos, utter confusion

My Benediction (= Good Words) to You

AT THE END OF THE DAY—AND BY THAT I MEAN **the** day—the only things we have are our relationships with other people and our relationship with God. Everything else will be gone.

With that in mind—now and always—let's cultivate those relationships.

As we close this chapter of our lives and open up ourselves to new people and new experiences, let us keep these words in mind. The author is unknown, but the advice is universal:

Life is short
And we don't have much time to gladden the hearts of those who travel with us,
So let us be swift to love,
Make haste to be kind,
And go in peace to love and serve the Lord.
Amen!

About the Author

AFTER FORTY YEARS of marriage, Holly found herself in the throes of a divorce, searching for a path through those turbulent times. Soon she found inspiring messages coming to her just when she needed them. Approaching the subject with honesty and humor, Holly wrote these essays over the next several years.

This book is the compilation of these messages over the span of the next four years. Holly decided that she wanted to publish them, so that others might find the strength to see their way through to better times.

A retired ordained minister in the United Church of Christ, Holly graduated from Wells College in 1978 with a B.A. in Psychology. In 1981she graduated with a Master's of Divinity degree from Princeton Theological Seminary with a concentration in Preaching. Holly has served congregations in NY state and Vermont and currently supplies pulpits in various churches in the area near where she lives.

Holly has two grown sons (and their significant others), 5 grandchildren, and lives with her greyhound in rural Vermont. She loves to knit, kayak, spend time with family, and travel with friends.

www.ingramcontent.com/pod-product-compliance
Lightning Source LLC
LaVergne TN
LVHW051842080426
835512LV00018B/3031